EXTREME
BALLOON
TYING

MORE THAN
40
OVER-THE-TOP
PROJECTS

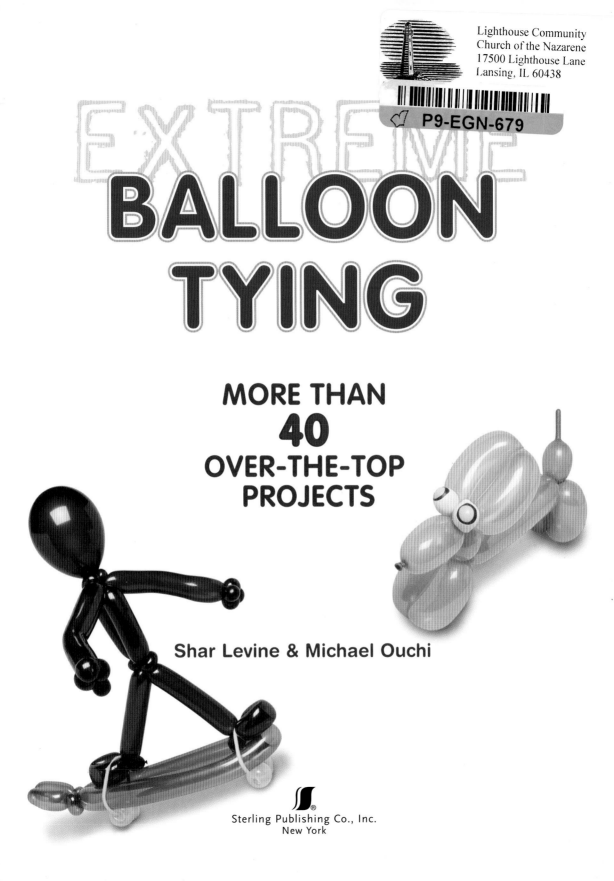

Shar Levine & Michael Ouchi

Sterling Publishing Co., Inc.
New York

FOR Giezelle and Michael Pash, Nicky and Ray Bergen, Jeff Connery and Cyndy Brown, and Maryann Cummings and Jonathan Rubinstein. Thank you all for being my friends, even though I am undeserving of your kindness and generosity. —Shar

FOR my son Malcolm (who loves to take the balloons apart), my son Maxwell, and my wife Tracy, all of whom support me in my many adventures. —Michael

Acknowledgments

We would like to thank Leslie Johnstone for the loan of her digital camera and for her friendship and support. We are also most grateful to Jared, Jessie, Gabriel, Alexander, and Christopher for the removal of all the balloon creations. Without your help, we would be waist-deep in twisted animals. We would also like to thank Michelle Gerber for taking care of the "boys" during the photo shoot.

Thanks to Berkeley Breathed for his kindness. A special thanks to Julie Conner of the Pioneer Balloon Company for providing the dragon sculpture photo from the International Balloon Arts Convention, permission, and information. The sculpture was designed by Rocky Toomey, CBA, of Future Affairs Productions, Inc., Providence, RI, and took 43 artists 881 hours and 18,876 Qualatex balloons to build.

Photography: Jeff Connery
Illustrations: Mario Ferro
Book Design: Rachel Maloney

Library of Congress Cataloging-in-Publication Data
Levine, Shar, 1953-
   Extreme balloon tying : more than 40 over-the-top projects / Shar Levine & Michael Ouchi.
      p. cm.
   Includes index.
   ISBN-13: 978-1-4027-2465-7
   ISBN-10: 1-4027-2465-9
   1. Balloon sculpture. I. Ouchi, Michael. II. Title.

TT926.L4779 2006
745.594—dc22

2006007319

1 2 3 4 5 6 7 8 9 10

Published by Sterling Publishing Co., Inc.
387 Park Avenue South, New York, NY 10016
© 2006 by Shar Levine and Michael Ouchi

Distributed in Canada by Sterling Publishing
c/o Canadian Manda Group, 165 Dufferin Street
Toronto, Ontario, Canada M6K 3H6

Distributed in the United Kingdom by GMC Distribution Services,
Castle Place, 166 High Street, Lewes, East Sussex, England BN7 1XU

Distributed in Australia by Capricorn Link (Australia) Pty. Ltd.
P.O. Box 704, Windsor, NSW 2756, Australia

Sterling ISBN-13: 987-1-4027-2465-7
          ISBN-10: 1-4027-2465-9

For information about custom editions, special sales, premium and corporate purchases,
please contact Sterling Special Sales Department at 800-805-5489 or specialsales@sterlingpub.com.

CONTENTS

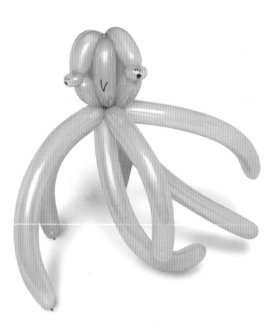

*Either small glow sticks are part of the project or they can be added.

INTRODUCTION

Extreme sports,
like white water rafting, skydiving, or
rock climbing, can be dangerous and
difficult. You need special training,
equipment, and the courage to put
your life on the line. But extreme
ballooning is something everyone
can do. You won't be exposed to any
life-threatening situations, and the
only thing you may break is a simple
balloon. This is not to say that blowing
balloon sculptures is pedestrian. On

the contrary, the creations in this book will challenge and impress even the most experienced
balloon artist.

Novice, or beginner, balloon blowers need not worry. You have to walk before you can run, or
in this case, blow up a balloon and tie it correctly before you can make a balloon creation, so
there will be a review of the basics.

As with most skills, it will take time and practice until you can make a perfect sculpture, and
you are bound to make lots of strange-looking creatures along the way. But keep trying and soon
you will become an expert balloonist.

Some creations in this book are a snap and will take just a few minutes to twist. OK—only
a few minutes when you know what you are doing. Many of the extreme sculptures will not
only take practice but also a bit of time. Expect to take a half hour or more on the weaves
and baskets. And, with the large creations, it is helpful to have a pump, as you can get pretty
light-headed blowing up loads of balloons.

Each of the projects in this book is rated on a scale of 1 to 5, with 1 being the easiest and
5 being the most difficult. Therefore, you may want to work on the easier projects before
advancing to the more challenging ones. And, unless instructed otherwise, you will be using
260, or animal entertainer, balloons for all of the creations.

PART I
Materials, Safety Tips & Techniques

Chapter 1

Materials

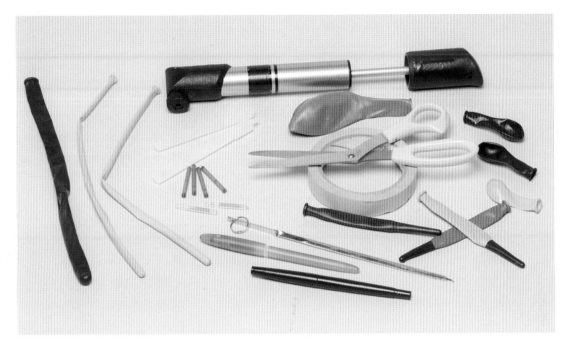

Did you know that there are different kinds of balloons? Balloons come in all shapes and sizes. Some are perfect for being inflated with helium. Some are used as decorations for parties and celebrations. Others are meant for making all kinds of creations.

For the creations in this book, you will need
• Balloons
• Animal entertainer, or 260 balloons
• Bee body, or 321, balloons*
• Airship, or 350, specialty balloons*
• Round balloons* (6-, 9-, and 11-inch plain colored)
• Balloon hand pump (optional)
• Scissors
• Metal turkey skewer
• Felt-tip pen with non-alcohol ink
• Adult helper
• Ribbons of various colors and thicknesses (optional)
• Glow sticks (available at discount stores, specialty toy stores, or in seasonal departments around Halloween)

• Small round bells (optional)
• Rice
• Funnel or plastic pop bottle
• Masking or duct tape

*The names of some balloons vary, depending on the manufacturer and the size of the balloon.

Types of Balloon

Long, skinny balloons are usually identified by a three-digit number (for example, 260). The first digit indicates the diameter (in inches) of a fully inflated balloon. The following two digits refer to the length (also in inches) of the fully inflated balloon.

So, our 260 balloon example will inflate up to 2 inches in width and 60 inches in length. Sometimes, however, you can end up with a large variation of sizes when you use the same type of balloon. Even within the same package, you'll find that different colors inflate to different sizes.

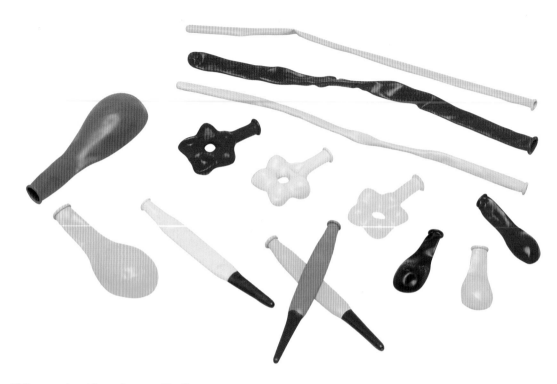

Where to Purchase Balloons

The balloons you are probably most familiar with are the kind you get in bags from a toy or department store. The bag may contain 25 balloons of different shapes and sizes. These are not the balloons to use for the creations in this book. You will need to use balloons specifically manufactured for twisting and turning. These balloons can be ordered over the Internet or purchased in party and novelty stores. The less expensive the balloon, the more likely it is to break. Saving a few pennies may not be worth it in the long run if the balloon is fragile and pops easily.

Storing Balloons

Balloons have a life. OK—not much of a life, because they can't go to movies or play sports. But you can treat your balloons in such a way as to extend their "life." Latex, the material these balloons are made from, is sensitive to sunlight. Leaving your balloons out on the counter or on a shelf in your bedroom will affect them. To make your balloons last longer, fold them into a sealable plastic bag and place this bag into an insulated lunch container, or find a safe spot for this bag in your refrigerator. This keeps the balloons cold, dry, and away from light.

Here's a simple experiment to prove this point. Take two 260 balloons and stretch one balloon over a coat hanger, tying it in place. Leave the hanger with the balloon outside in the sun for several days. Take the second balloon and place it in a sealable plastic bag. Place this bag in a dark container and leave this in the refrigerator. After a few days, place the balloons side by side and stretch them. What happened to the one that was in the sun?

Chapter 2

Techniques

Here are some simple terms you need to know before you begin learning the techniques.

Bubble: The inflated portion of a balloon formed between two twists.

Mouth: The part of the balloon you put your lips over to blow up the balloon.

Tail: The rounded end, or tip, of the balloon.

Joint: The thin piece of latex created from a twist.

Twist: The turning, or rotating, of a balloon that will form a bubble and a joint.

Balloon puff: A special bubble formed in the tail of a blown balloon.

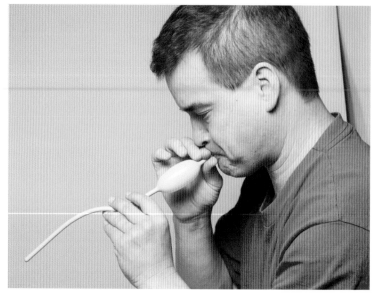

Inflating Balloons

Professional balloonists make blowing up balloons look so simple. It is easy for them, but it's going to take some practice to become that easy for you. There are a number of tricks to blowing up a long, thin balloon.

Hold the ends of the balloon, and give the balloon a quick stretch to loosen it up. Use the thumb and index finger of one hand to squeeze the balloon about 1 inch (2.5 cm) from the opening. With your other hand, hold the mouth of the balloon between your lips, and blow up just the 1-inch (2.5-cm) section of the balloon. As you continue to blow, pull the balloon away from you with the hand squeezing the balloon. When you have a small bubble of air, stop there and take a deep breath. Now, blow into the balloon as you slowly pull your fingers down the balloon. This stretches the balloon and makes it easier for you to inflate it.

Do not fill your cheeks with air and make a face that looks like a puffer fish! You don't want to blow with your cheeks! Instead, blow air from your diaphragm. Right now you're probably looking around your body trying to find your diaphragm. Put your hand a couple of inches above your navel. Your diaphragm is inside there.

Depending on the thickness and length of the balloon, it may take several breaths to fill the balloon completely. Do not try to blow up the entire balloon with one breath! Always leave at least an inch or two at the tail, or tip, of the balloon. This gives the air in the balloon somewhere to go when you are pushing and twisting it.

Plan B: Using a Pump

Even professional balloon artists get winded after blowing up balloons all day. A simple air pump can come to the rescue.

Place the open end of the balloon over the nozzle of the pump. Hold the balloon firmly in place with one hand, and use your other hand to pull the plunger back. Push the plunger back and forth to pump the air into the balloon. It will take several pumps to inflate the balloon.

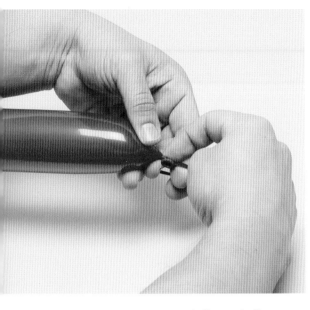

There is a tendency to overinflate a balloon with a pump, so don't get too ambitious when pumping in air.

Burping

Babies get burped after they are fed, but did you know that balloons also get burped? After you inflate a balloon to the desired length, let out just a squeak of air. This is called burping the balloon. It is really important to do this, as it will soften the balloon. If the balloon is too firm, it will be difficult to twist and may even pop.

Tying a Balloon

Once you've inflated the balloon and burped it to make it soft, then comes the challenge of securing the air inside. Wrap the mouth end of the balloon around your index and middle fingers. This creates a ridge area. Use the index finger on your free hand to fold the mouth of the balloon through the ridge area. Pull it through and the balloon with snap shut.

When the instructions say to inflate or fully inflate a balloon, it is presumed that you will blow up the balloon and tie the end so that the air doesn't get out. Therefore, the directions don't always include the part about tying off.

Note to Balloon Twisters: Remember, unless otherwise specified, all balloons used in making these creations are 260's.

Safety Tips

Before you start learning the various techniques in making your creations, you should be aware of the following precautions.

Do's and Don'ts

Here are some simple rules to follow to make sure that your balloon-making experience is safe and fun:

- Store your balloons in a cool, dry place away from the sun. They will last longer this way.
- Do not chew on balloons or place balloons in your mouth!
- Do not blow up a balloon that another person has already been blowing. You can pick up some nasty germs this way.
- Do not use helium to inflate these balloons. It's a waste of helium and the creatures won't float.
- Unless instructed, do not put any materials inside the balloons.
- Unless instructed, do not use regular round balloons to make these creations. These balloons are not meant for twisting and will burst.
- Do not use alcohol-based felt-tip pens to draw on your balloons. These pens will eat through the balloon.
- Even if you've seen a professional balloon artist inflating the tail of a balloon by putting the tail in his or her mouth and pulling out the balloon puff, do not attempt to do this! It is easy to choke on a balloon.
- Use a turkey skewer or pin to prick balloons. Do not use your teeth to puncture them.
- Make sure you pick up all burst balloon pieces. Small children and animals could swallow them.

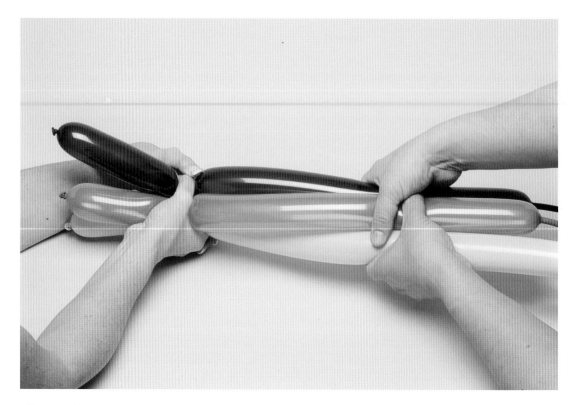

• Tell an adult immediately if you have hurt
  yourself or a friend in any way!

Other Precautions

Balloons can pop. If balloons pop too close to
your eyes, the flying pieces can snap back and
really hurt you! When blowing up a balloon, it
is recommended that you cup the palm of your
hand over the top of the balloon. This way, if
the balloon pops, you are less likely to get
stung by flying latex. As silly as it may look, you
can wear swim goggles or even safety goggles
to protect your eyes from bursting balloons. In
fact, this is probably a pretty good idea,
especially if you are a beginner. When you are
twisting a balloon, keep the balloon far away
from your face to avoid any similar accidents.

Sometimes you may find it difficult to hold
more than one balloon at a time. Ask a friend
to hold one end of the balloon while you twist
and turn the other balloons.

Balloons break. Life's like that. Even the most
expert balloonist breaks the occasional balloon
while twisting the latex to make a creation. But
don't be afraid to give the balloons a good
twist, and do wear safety eyewear.

This may seem obvious, but you'll probably
want to have short fingernails when you make
these creations. Use a nail file to round off
rough edges of your nails. Some professionals
use a squirt of hand lotion to soften their
hands before twisting balloons.

Finally, remember that practice makes perfect.
It's difficult to be able to twist balloons to be
exactly the same size. The more you work at the
creations, the easier all the aspects will be.

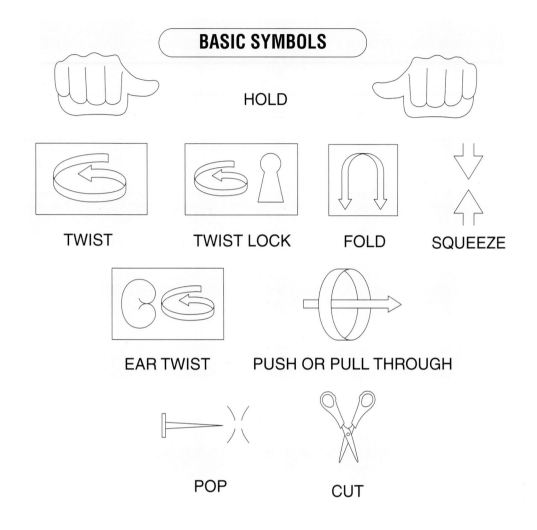

BASIC SYMBOLS

HOLD

TWIST

TWIST LOCK

FOLD

SQUEEZE

EAR TWIST

PUSH OR PULL THROUGH

POP

CUT

Basic Twists

Now that you have an inflated balloon, what can you do with it? You could hold it up proudly and tell your family you've made a snake. Or, you can twist and turn this colorful balloon and make something truly amazing.

Strange as it might seem, there is a front part and a back part of a balloon. Always begin your twists at the mouth (knotted) end of the balloon. This allows the air forced out on each twist to move to the tail end of the balloon. If you have left enough space at the tail, the balloon won't pop.

When twisting balloons, make sure you always turn them in the same direction—that is, all clockwise or all counterclockwise. If you change the directions of the turns, the balloon will untwist itself and you'll be right back where you started!

BASIC TWIST

The first basic twist (also called a basic twist) is the first twist you need to learn in balloon crafting.

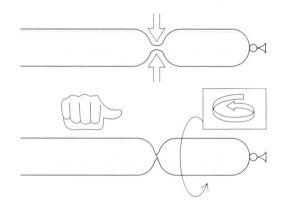

1 Squeeze the balloon to the desired size.

2 Use one hand to hold the end of the balloon, while the other hand twists the balloon in three or more full rotations.

- A very small balloon twist makes a bubble that is approximately ½ inch (1.25 cm) long.
- A small balloon twist makes a bubble less than 1 inch (2.5 cm) long.
- A medium balloon twist makes a bubble between 1½ and 2 inches (4 and 5 cm) long.

- A large balloon twist makes a bubble approximately 2 to 3 inches (5 to 7.5 cm) long.

When making several balloon bubbles in a row, remember to hold on to the first and last balloon bubble. This isn't easy and may require either help from someone or the use of other parts of your body, such as your toes, knees, or elbows.

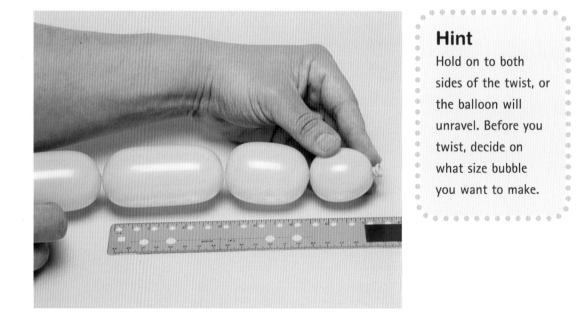

TWIST LOCK

Now that you can blow up and twist a balloon, how do you get those bubbles to stay in place?

1 Make a small bubble, followed by two medium bubbles. Remember to hold the first and last bubble, or you'll be doing this again.

2 Place the two medium bubbles side by side by folding at the twisted point, or joint, where they connect.

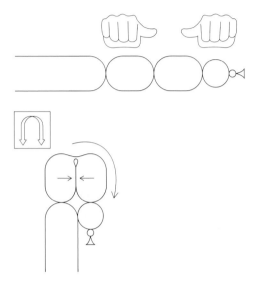

3 Gently pull up the twisted bubbles and twist them around their bottom joints. Twist at least three times. This will hold the medium bubbles in place.

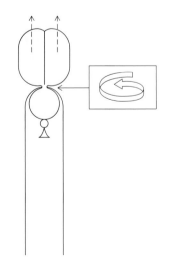

EAR TWIST

This special twist is perfect for creating ears, a nose, or elbows on your balloon creatures.

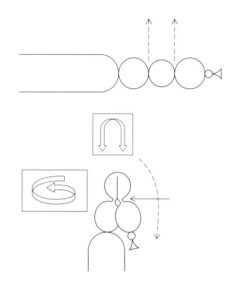

1 Make three bubbles: a small bubble, a smaller bubble (less than 1 inch long), and another small bubble the same size as the first one.

2 Pull up on the tiny middle bubble at the joints, while holding or squeezing the two small bubbles together. Twist the middle bubble three times. This will make the tiny bubble into an elbow.

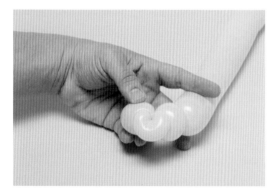

3 To turn this bubble into an ear, grab the bubble with your fingers and use your thumb to lay the bubble down on its side. You can also rotate this bubble to form a nose.

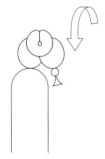

Hint

When making the ear twists with the small bubbles, fold the two halves of the balloon toward each other and have the middle bubble facing away from the fold. Move, or rotate, the segmented section after each twist.

FOLD TWIST

A fold twist is the same as an ear twist, except that you use a large bubble in the center instead of a tiny one.

1 Twist a small bubble and a large bubble.

2 Pull up on the large bubble and fold it in half. Squeeze the small bubble and the rest of the balloon together. Twist the middle bubble three times.

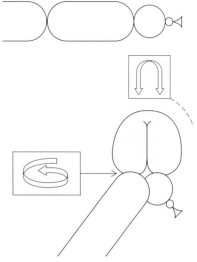

TULIP TWIST

This twist will take some practice. Use a clear balloon when you are learning so that you can see the knot through the balloon.

1 Hold a blown balloon several inches from the tied mouth end. Use the tip of your longest finger to poke the knot into the balloon. Keep forcing the knot down until it is one or two knuckles inside the balloon.

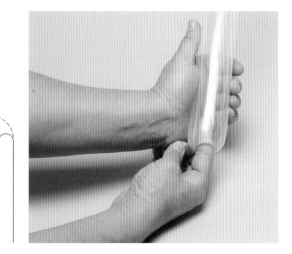

2 With your free hand, grab hold of the knot and then pull your finger out of the balloon.

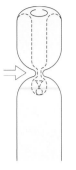 

3 Pull up on the bulb of the "tulip" and twist the balloon, making sure the knot is below the twist with the remainder of the balloon.

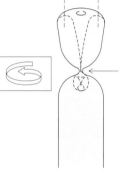 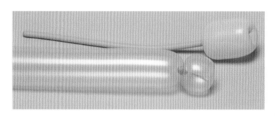

POP TWIST

What do you think will happen if a bubble pops while you are twisting a balloon? You'll be pleasantly surprised with this twist. When creating a pop twist, you generally need to make an uneven number of bubbles.

1 Make a medium bubble and then a series of five small bubbles. Twist the first and last bubbles together to form a ring of bubbles. The bubbles next to the pop twist bubble are usually small bubbles.

2 Pull up on the second bubble and make an ear twist.

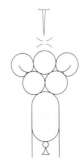

3 Do the same thing to the fourth bubble. This seals off the middle (pop twist) bubble.

4 Use a pin, turkey skewer, or bamboo skewer to poke a hole in the middle bubble. If you have done your twisting correctly, the first, second, fourth, and fifth bubbles will still be inflated, but there will be two separate sides.

Hint

Pop twist balloon creations are symmetrical. This means that you have to twist an equal number of bubbles for each side. This technique will be used in the Starfish, for example (see page 38).

BALLOON PUFF

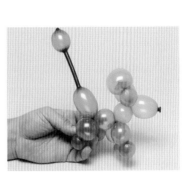

This puff seems to appear like magic at the end of a blown balloon. Do not try to do this technique by putting the tail in your mouth! This is a difficult technique and may take a lot of practice.

1 Pull the tail several times to loosen it. Then cup your hand around the inflated part of the balloon where the tail begins.

2 Squeeze the air from the inflated section into the tail section.

3 Adjust the size of the bubble by squeezing air from the puff section.

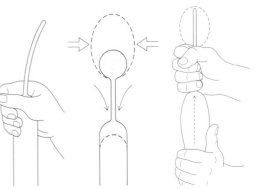

More Twists

Note: The following twists, as well as each of the projects in this book, are rated on a scale of 1 to 5, with 1 being the easiest and 5 being the most difficult.

ROLL LOCK
Level of Difficulty: 1

1 Make a medium bubble and then a second medium bubble. Twist lock these bubbles together.

2 Make a slightly smaller medium bubble, and push it through the joined bubbles.

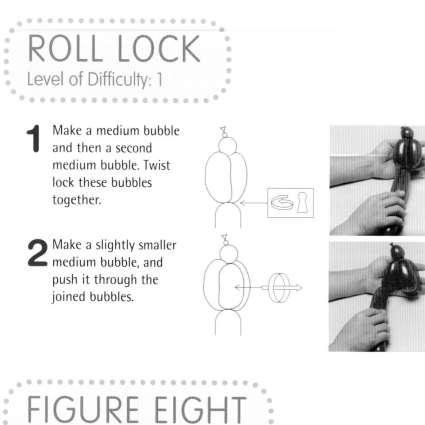

FIGURE EIGHT
Level of Difficulty: 1

You will be using this twist for many of the creations in this book.

1 Inflate a balloon. (If you are using a fully inflated balloon for your creation, be sure to burp the balloon before tying it off.)

2 Squeeze the tail to give it a slightly larger end. Tie the tail to the mouth.

3 You now have a large circular balloon. Hold the balloon at the tied end with the fingers of one hand, and run your other hand across to find the midpoint of the opposite side of the balloon. Pull the two points together and twist. You should now have something that resembles a figure eight.

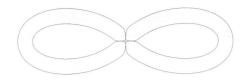

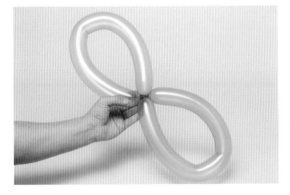

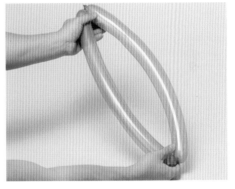

MIDPOINT TWIST
Level of Difficulty: 1

As you will see, the midpoint twist is just like the figure eight at the beginning, but then you do something different at the end.

1 Inflate a balloon. (If you are using a fully inflated balloon for your creation, burp the balloon before tying it off.)

2 Squeeze the tail to give it a slightly larger end. Tie the tail to the mouth.

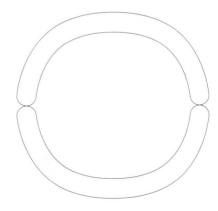

3 You now have a large circular balloon. Hold the balloon at the tied end with the fingers of one hand, and run your other hand across to find the midpoint of the opposite side of the balloon. Instead of pulling this point across and twisting to join the tied end, roll or twist the point, dividing your balloon into two equal halves.

GOOGLE EYES
Level of Difficulty: 5

This is one balloon twist right off the difficulty scale. It should be designated with a skull and crossbones. You will need three different colored balloons. We will use blue, red, and white here, but you can choose your own combinations for your creatures.

1 Partially inflate the blue balloon. Make a small bubble at the mouth end, and twist it several times to be sure that the air can't escape. Push the bubble inside the balloon with your finger, and grab it with your other hand. As you pull your finger out, twist it to the side to break the small bubble off the balloon. Use a pin to poke a hole in the tail of the balloon. Cut off the excess latex. You have a tiny bubble.

2 Partially inflate the red balloon and tie off. Push the tied end of the blue bubble into the knotted end of the red balloon. The red balloon should just about surround the blue bubble, allowing only a bit of it to show through. Deflate the red balloon with a turkey skewer. It will form a skin around the blue bubble. Trim off the end of the red balloon.

3 Partially inflate the white balloon and tie off. Push the tied end of the blue/red bubble into the knotted end of the white balloon. The white balloon should just about surround the blue/red bubble, allowing only a bit of it to show through. Deflate the white balloon with the skewer. It will form a skin around the other bubbles. Leave the excess latex to attach to your creature.

4 Make a second eyeball the same way you did in Steps 1-3.

DOG WITH GOOGLE EYES

Level of Difficulty: 5

To see how these google eyes can be incorporated into a creature, try this simple project.

BALLOON PROPORTIONS

1 Inflate a balloon, leaving about 6 inches (15 cm) free at the tail end. Twist a medium bubble. This is the head. Twist two more medium bubbles. These are the ears. Twist lock the second and third bubbles together. Your dog has a face.

2 Make a small bubble and hold on to it until it is joined to the legs. This is the neck. Then twist two medium bubbles. These are the legs. Twist lock them to the neck, and then adjust the bubbles so that they are aligned to form the head, ears, and front feet of the dog.

3 Make a twist about 5 inches (12.5 cm) from the front legs. This is the body. Then twist two medium bubbles the same size as the front legs. Twist lock the back legs to the body. The remaining part of the balloon forms the tail, which holds the back legs in place.

4 Here's the cool part. Tie the ends of the google eyes together, and wrap the ends around the ears. Adjust the eyes to the desired length, and cut off the ends of the white balloon.

ROUND EYES
Level of Difficulty: 1

This is one of the few times you can twist a round balloon. For certain creations in this book, you will be using a 6-, 9-, or 11-inch round balloon

1 Inflate the round balloon until it is half to three-quarters full, leaving the balloon soft enough to twist.

2 Hold the balloon with the knot facing downward, and place your hands so that your fingers wrap around the balloon from top to bottom. Squeeze the balloon and twist to create two halves. These are giant "eyes."

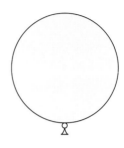

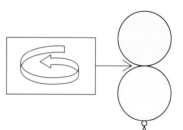

Hint
You can add two small glow sticks to the eyes and twist, making sure one glow stick is on each side (see page 87).

RAISIN TWIST
Level of Difficulty: 4

This twist makes it look as if you've glued a balloon onto the surface of another balloon. How is this possible?

1 For each balloon you want to "attach" to the surface of a round balloon, you will need a wad of latex. To make this wad, find a length of burst balloon and tie several knots in the balloon to create a roundish blob. Drop this wad into an uninflated round balloon.

2 Inflate the round balloon only about three-quarters of the way, making sure to leave the balloon soft enough to twist. Locate the space where you want to attach the twisted balloon, and tip the round balloon so that the wad moves there.

3 Pinch the wad between your fingers, and pull it toward you, twisting so that it forms something that resembles a raisin (hence, the name). Twist whatever shape you want to attach to this raisin, and it will stay on the surface of the round balloon.

Weaves

Weaving with balloons produces the most spectacular sculptures. Sadly, these decorations can take an hour or more to make and will eat up a lot of balloons. However, they are not that difficult to make, just time-consuming.

The good news: If one of the balloons in your weave breaks, you can simply blow up another balloon and tie it in!

STARBURST
Level of Difficulty: 3

This makes an amazing weave, which will take about 15 minutes, but the effort is worth it. To avoid confusion when you are learning this technique, you might want to use balloons of different colors for the spokes and the weave. Here, we are using white for the spokes and various other colors for the weave.

1 Fully inflate five white balloons, burp out a small amount of air, and tie the balloons together at the knots. These are the spokes of the starburst.

2 Take one of the balloon spokes and make a small bubble near the twist and ear twist. This bubble will help to keep your starburst flat.

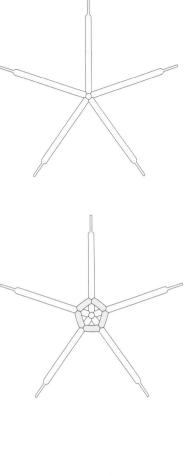

3 Inflate a balloon in a different color, leaving 3 to 4 inches (7.5 to 10 cm) uninflated at the tail. This balloon will be used for the weave and will be attached to the spoke. Make a small-to-medium bubble in the weave balloon, and twist lock this bubble to the spoke bubble. Repeat this step on the next spoke, measuring the weave bubble against the previous weave bubble to ensure they are the same size. This way, your starburst will be flat. Continue repeating this step until you have gone around the spokes. Deflate the excess balloon with a turkey skewer and tie it off after you have completed one rotation.

4 Start the next row on the spoke by repeating Step 3 with a different-colored balloon. Keep the spoke bubbles the same size, but make the weave bubbles slightly larger than the previous row. The goal is to have the starburst lay flat. For example, the size of the first row's weave bubble could be 1 inch (2.5 cm), the second row 2 inches (5 cm), the third row 4 inches (10 cm), etc. After several rows, your weave balloon may be too short to complete a full rotation. If this is the case, inflate another balloon to complete the row, and then deflate. Continue adding more weaves and rows until your starburst is the size you want it to be.

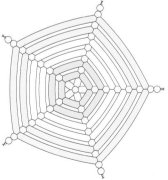

HANGING BASKET
Level of Difficulty: 4

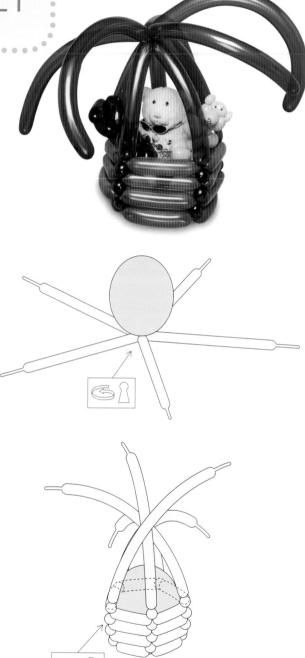

This is the perfect sculpture for suspending balloon flowers or small balloon animals.

1 Follow the basic directions for making the starburst above. But instead of trying to make all the weaves lay flat, the goal is to get them to curve. Now inflate an 11-inch round balloon. Tie the five inflated spoke balloons together, and twist these to the knot at the end of the round balloon. Use the round balloon as a frame to help you determine the size of the weave balloons.

2 Follow the steps for making a starburst, but this time make the weaves longer so that they begin to curve. Follow the contours of the round balloon to shape your basket. When the round balloon begins to arc, or curve inward, start making the weave balloons shorter. Your basket will begin to take on a curved shape.

3 After about six rows, gather the spokes together. Pop the round balloon and remove, leaving a basket. Suspend from the ceiling, and fill with balloon animals, balloon fruit, balloon flowers, or even soft toys.

VASE
Level of Difficulty: 3

This vase makes a great container for a potted plant, or you can fill it with balloon fruit.

1 Inflate four balloons, leaving 4 inches (10 cm) uninflated at the tail, and tie the knots together. Take one of the balloon spokes, and make a small bubble near the twist.

2 For each spoke, go down about 4 inches from the twist and make a small bubble and ear twist to close. This will build a vase or basket with straight sides.

3 Inflate the weave balloon, leaving 4 inches free at the tail. Attach it to the spokes the same way you did for the Starburst and Hanging Basket, but this time make all the weaves on the spoke the same size. Use the balloon in the row below as a template for the weave balloon in the next row. They will not grow larger as they did with the Starburst. The goal is to make a flat four-sided vase.

4 When the vase has reached the desired length, you can make a small bubble and ear twist to close. Deflate and tie off. Do not fill it with anything that has sharp edges, like real flowers. Balloon flowers look great in this container.

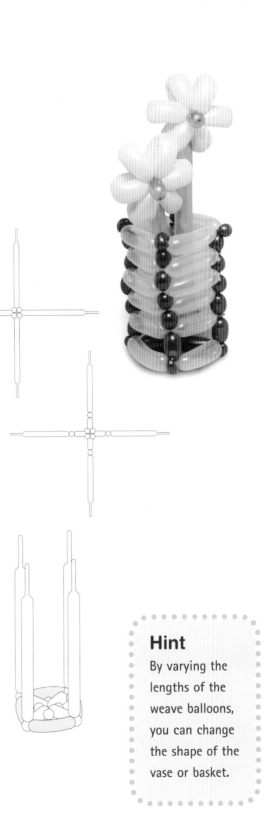

Hint
By varying the lengths of the weave balloons, you can change the shape of the vase or basket.

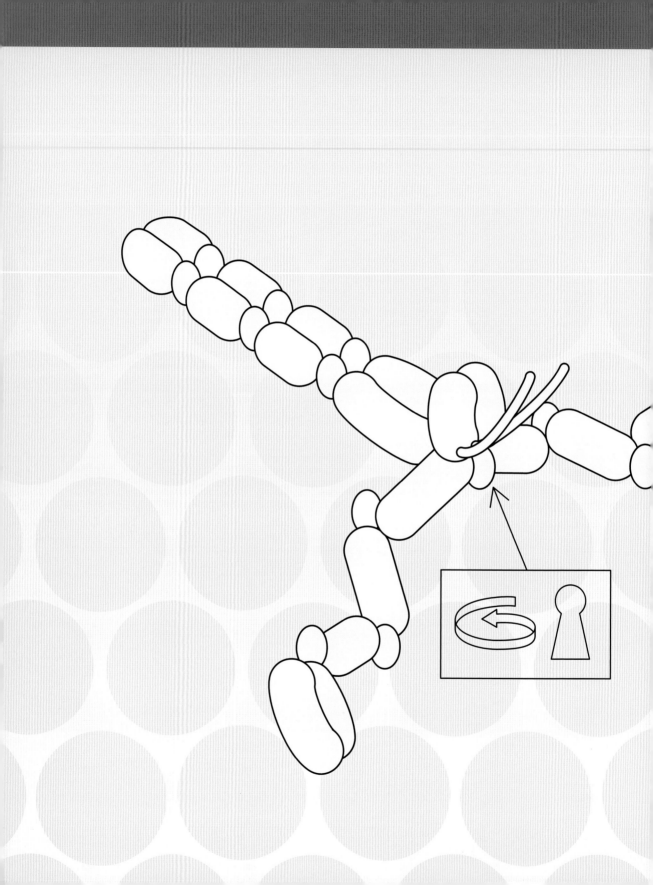

PART II
Balloon Creatures

Chapter 3

Creature Features

LOBSTER
Level of Difficulty: 2

Here's one crustacean you can't enjoy with drawn butter. You will need three red balloons for this project.

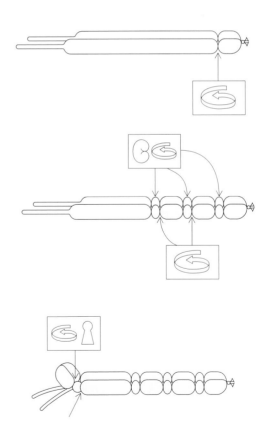

BALLOON PROPORTIONS

Body

1 Inflate two of the balloons, leaving 6 to 8 inches (15 to 20 cm) uninflated at the tail end. Tie the knotted ends of these balloons together.

2 Holding the balloons together, make a twist with both balloons about 3 inches (7.5 cm) down from the end.

3 Make a small bubble with the two balloons, and ear twist them together. Lay them flat to the 3-inch bubbles.

4 Repeat Steps 2 and 3 two more times.

5 Holding the balloons together, make a 6-inch bubble and twist lock. You will have two bubbles left over. Choosing the larger of the two, make two 1-inch (2.5-cm) bubbles and twist lock them together. This creates the eyes. For the smaller one, make a small bubble, ear twist, and deflate and tie off.

Claws

6 Inflate the third balloon, leaving 5 to 6 inches (12.5 to 15 cm) free at the tail end.

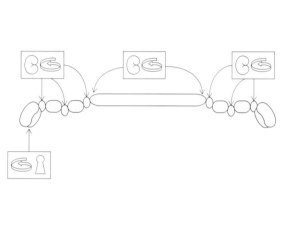

7 Make a very small bubble and wrap the knot around the twist and ear twist. Make a small bubble and then a medium bubble, and twist lock them together. This forms the claw. Make a 2-inch (5-cm) bubble, very small bubble, and ear twist. Make another 2-inch bubble, very small bubble, and ear twist.

8 Make a 3-inch bubble.

9 Repeat Steps 7 and 8 in reverse: 3-inch bubble (the 3-inch bubbles may untwist, which won't be a problem), very small bubble, and ear twist; 2-inch bubble, very small bubble, and ear twist; and another 2-inch bubble, very small bubble, and ear twist.

To make the other claw, you make a small bubble and, with the remaining balloon section, twist a small bubble at the end and twist lock that bubble to the small bubble.

10 Twist lock the midpoint of the balloon section, and wrap this part around the head.

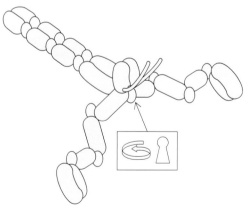

CRAB
Level of Difficulty: 2

Make this the next time you are in a "crabby" mood.

CRAB BALLOON PROPORTIONS

1 Inflate two balloons to equal lengths, leaving about 8 inches (20 cm) uninflated at the tail end.

2 Starting with one balloon, make a small bubble and medium bubble, and twist lock them together. Then make a very small bubble and ear twist it. These are the claws. Repeat this step using the second balloon.

3 Hold both balloons together with the claws facing outward. Grab the balloons about 2 inches (5 cm) down and twist lock them together.

4 On one balloon, make a medium bubble, small bubble, ear twist, medium bubble, small bubble, and ear twist. Repeat on the second side. After a small bubble, grab both balloons together and twist lock them.

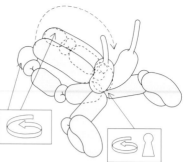

5 Fold the remaining balloon sections over the back side of the body, and twist lock at the point where the claws are located.

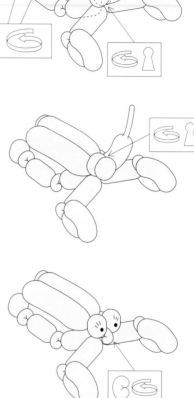

6 To create the eyes, use one of the balloon sections and make two small bubbles, folding them over and twist locking.

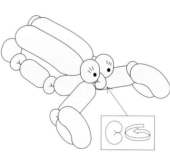

7 Using another balloon section, make a small bubble and ear twist it, and then pop the end with a turkey skewer, tying off to complete. Pull the ear twist bubble between the two claws, and adjust all the bubbles to look like a crab. Draw on a face with a felt-tip pen. Adjust the claws to face inward.

DOLPHIN
Level of Difficulty: 3

This creature is created from the tail to the front.

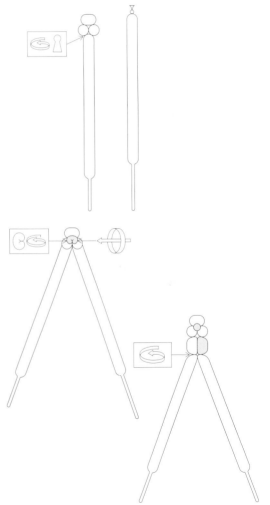

BALLOON PROPORTIONS

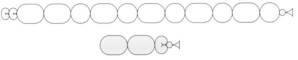

1 Inflate a blue balloon and a white balloon, leaving about 4 to 5 inches (10 to 12.5 cm) uninflated at the tail end.

2 Starting with the blue balloon, make a small bubble, medium bubble, and another small bubble. Tie the knot around the third bubble. You should now have a triangle.

3 Make a small bubble on the white balloon, and fold the knot over to make an ear twist. Twist lock the white balloon to the blue balloon at the last joint. Force the white ear-twisted bubble through the space in the blue balloon between the medium and small bubbles.

4 Adjust the balloons so that the blue balloon is on top of the white one. Gather the balloons together and twist them to make a medium bubble.

5 Using only the blue balloon, make a small bubble and medium bubble, and twist lock them together. Repeat this step two more times to make the fins and flippers.

6 Using the blue balloon, make a 2-inch (5-cm) bubble and two small bubbles, and twist lock the two small bubbles. Ear twist the small bubbles to form the lips. Deflate the blue balloon with a turkey skewer and tie off, wrapping the excess latex around a joint.

7 Wrap the last joint on the blue balloon to the white balloon and twist. Deflate the white balloon with the skewer and tie off. Cut off the excess with scissors.

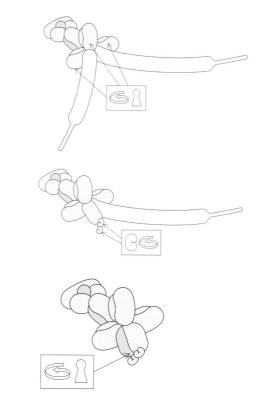

ORCA OR KILLER WHALE
Level of Difficulty: 3

Killer whales, also known as orcas, are beautiful creatures found along the west coast of Canada and the Pacific Northwest of the United States, but you can find one in your bag of balloons. Make several of these and you will have your own "pod."

1 To make a killer whale, repeat the instructions for the dolphin above, but use a black balloon instead of a blue one. Add a tape dot for eyes.

STARFISH
Level of Difficulty: 3

To paraphrase the great Dr. Seuss, one starfish, two starfish, red starfish, blue starfish. Here's how to make your own balloon starfish collection.

BALLOON PROPORTIONS

1 Inflate a balloon, leaving 6 inches (15 cm) uninflated at the tail end. Make a small bubble, twist, tie the knot over to hold in place, and then twist in half to make two very small bubbles.

2 Make a 4-inch (10 cm) bubble then make a small bubble and ear twist it for the center of the starfish. Make a 4-inch (10-cm) bubble. This is an "arm." Make three small bubbles and then a 4-inch bubble. Fold these over and twist lock the last bubble into the center. Repeat this step so that you now have five arms: four arms with double bubbles and one with a single bubble. If there is any extra balloon left over, pop it with a turkey skewer and tie the latex around the center bubble.

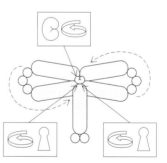

3 Ear twist the first and third bubbles on the arms, and use the skewer to pop the middle bubble (pop twist).

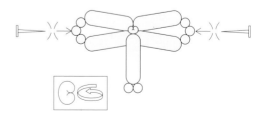

STARFISH 2
Level of Difficulty: 1

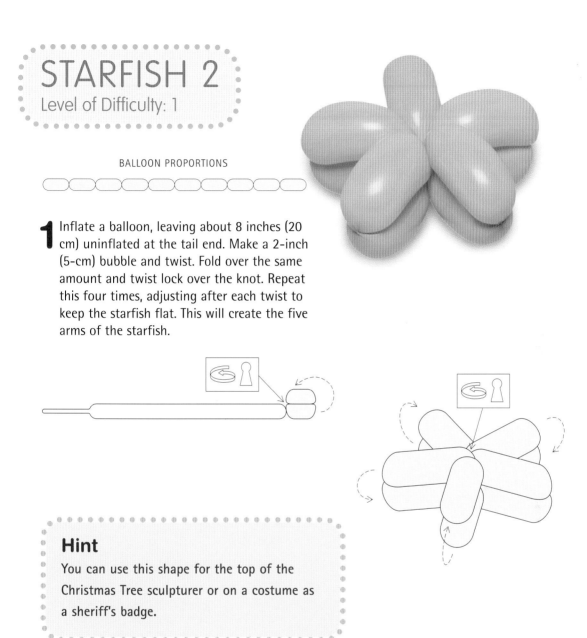

BALLOON PROPORTIONS

1 Inflate a balloon, leaving about 8 inches (20 cm) uninflated at the tail end. Make a 2-inch (5-cm) bubble and twist. Fold over the same amount and twist lock over the knot. Repeat this four times, adjusting after each twist to keep the starfish flat. This will create the five arms of the starfish.

Hint
You can use this shape for the top of the Christmas Tree sculpturer or on a costume as a sheriff's badge.

PENGUIN
Level of Difficulty: 3

Not only is this one-balloon penguin a cute creation, but you will also learn the hook twist. This creation is dedicated to Berkeley Breathed and Opus.

BALLOON PROPORTIONS

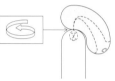

1 Start by inflating a black balloon, leaving about 8½ inches (21.25 cm) uninflated at the tail end.

2 The next part is tricky. To make a hook, you will use the same method as in the tulip twist, except this time you will hold the tied end on the side of the balloon, not in the middle. Push the knot as far into the balloon as your finger can reach. If you wish, ask an adult to help you, or you can scrunch up the balloon to get your finger in as far as you can go. Hold the knot on the side of the balloon and pull your finger out. Twist the balloon with the knot on the tail side of the balloon. This is the penguin's beak.

3 Make an 8-inch (20-cm) bubble, fold over, and then twist. Open the circle, and push the beak through the opening to hold it in place. This is the head.

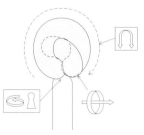

4 The body consists of three parts. Start by making two 3-inch (7.5-cm) bubbles and twist. Make a third 3-inch bubble, twist, and then roll lock (see page TK for the roll lock technique). You've got the body.

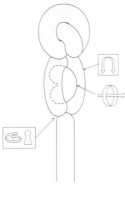

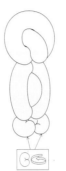

5 Make a 1½-inch (4-cm) bubble and ear twist, and then a second 1½-inch bubble and ear twist. These are the feet. You should have a small bit of blown balloon left over. Use a turkey skewer to pop this part of the balloon, and tie off the end.

BRONTOSAURUS
Level of Difficulty: 1

No one knows what color dinosaurs were, so let's make this one using three green balloons.

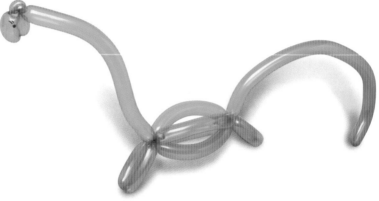

BALLOON PROPORTIONS

1 To make the body of the dinosaur, fully inflate one of the balloons and burp to soften it. Squeeze the tip of the tail end to remove some of the air, and make a midpoint twist. Pull this across and twist to make a figure eight. Fold the segments over each other, and push one section through.

2 To make the head, inflate the second balloon, leaving about 1 inch (2.5 cm) free at the tail end. Starting from the tied end, make a 1½-inch (4-cm) bubble and then a 3-inch (7.5-cm) bubble, and twist them together. Make a small bubble and ear twist to hold. Make another small bubble and ear twist, and you've got the head.

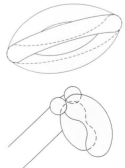

3 To make the front legs, start by squeezing the air to fill the tail of the balloon. Then create a small bubble at the tail end, followed by two 4-inch (10-cm) bubbles, and twist lock them together. Then push the small bubble through the two long bubbles to hold in place.

4 To join the body to the front legs, fold the small bubble on the legs through the front section of the body at the joint of the four bubbles and twist to lock in place. Adjust to make the bubbles symmetrical.

5 To make the back legs and tail, fully inflate the last balloon and burp a bit of air out. Make the same legs as you did for the front section by creating a small bubble starting at the knot end and then two 4-inch bubbles and twist lock them together. Then push the small bubble through the legs. Join the legs to the body as you did in Step 4.

6 Give the tail a curved look by bending and squeezing it in several places.

This is one dino that won't scare you. You will be using two balloons.

BALLOON PROPORTIONS

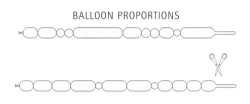

Head

1 Inflate the first balloon, leaving 3 to 4 inches (7.5 to 10 cm) uninflated at the tail end. Make a 1-inch (2.5-cm) bubble and then a 1½- to 2-inch (4- to 5-cm) bubble, and twist them together to lock in place. Make a small bubble and ear twist, and then twist the ear twist in half to make two separate eyes.

Body

2 Approximately 8 inches (20 cm) from the last twist, make a medium bubble, two small bubbles, and then another medium bubble, and twist lock these together. Then make a small bubble and ear twist, to lock the head and front legs in place. The remaining part of the balloon should now be inflated from this twisting.

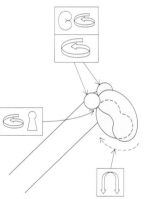

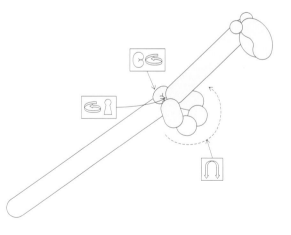

Legs

3 Inflate the second balloon, leaving about 4 to 5 inches (10 to 12.5 cm) free at the tail end. Starting from the tied end, make a small bubble and two medium bubbles, and then twist lock the two medium bubbles together. Make a 3-inch bubble and a very small bubble and ear twist. Then make a 3-inch bubble and twist, and a second 3-inch bubble and twist. Make a very small bubble and ear twist. The two 3-inch bubbles may untwist, which won't be a problem. Now make two 3-inch bubbles and twist lock them together, and make a very small bubble and twist. Then, holding at the last twist, use a turkey skewer to pop the bubble, and tie off at the end. Cut off the excess balloon with scissors.

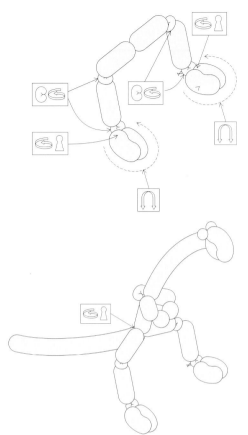

4 Now twist the legs in the middle of the long section, and join this to the front half of the dino several inches down from the front legs, and position the legs accordingly. Twist to hold in place.

5 Draw on teeth and eyes with a felt-tip pen.

SKATEBOARD
Level of Difficulty: 2

Don't try doing an ollie with this board. You'll need a blue balloon for the deck of the skateboard and two yellow or red balloons for the wheels.

BALLOON PROPORTIONS

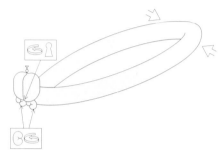

1 For the deck, start by fully inflating the blue balloon and burping it. Squeeze the tail end to move some of the air, and then tie the tail end to the mouth. Hold the tied ends with one hand, and make a medium twist about 2 inches (5 cm) down from the ends. Holding the tied ends together, make a small bubble and another small bubble and ear twist them together. This is one end of the deck.

2 Find the midpoint of the balloon, and use your hand to squeeze this together. It should form a rounded point.

3 Now for the wheels: Tie a knot in the tail end of the first yellow or red balloon. Inflate the balloon to about 2 to 3 inches (5 to 7.5 cm) and then tie off. Push the tied tail end of the balloon through the center of the balloon, as you would in a tulip twist. Pull your finger out and twist, making sure the knot is on the outside of the balloon.

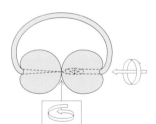

4 Push the knots back into the center of the balloon, and twist to create two small bubbles. The knots should be on the far side of the twist. Do not gather the uninflated part of the balloon in any of the twists.

5 Using the other yellow or red balloon, repeat Steps 3 and 4 to make the second set of wheels.

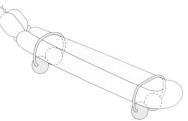

6 Taking the uninflated section of the two sets of wheels, slide the wheels over the deck.

SKATEBOARDER
Level of Difficulty: 3

How about an alien skateboarder? This figure can ride on the skateboard above.

BALLOON PROPORTIONS

1 Inflate two balloons, leaving 3 to 4 inches (7.5 to 10 cm) free at the tail end. Using one balloon, make a small bubble and add a fold twist bubble about 6 to 7 inches (15 to 17.5 cm) long. This is a foot. Repeat this step using the second balloon.

2 Hold the balloons together with the feet facing outward. Gather both balloons about 8 to 10 inches (20 to 25 cm) down from the last fold and twist lock them together.

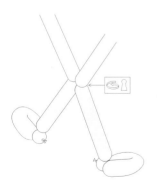

3 Using one balloon only, make a small bubble and ear twist it. Repeat on the second balloon. This creates the hips.

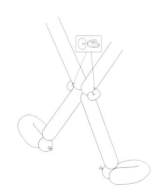

4 Gather both balloons about 5 inches (12.5 cm) down and twist lock them together.

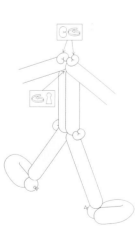

5 Repeat Step 3. This creates the shoulders.

6 Go down to the end of each remaining balloon section. Make four small bubbles, and twist lock the first and fourth bubbles on each balloon section.

7 Fully inflate a bee body (321) or round balloon and burp to soften it. If you used a bee body balloon, make a tulip twist and twist lock to join to the body using the stinger, or use the mouth to tie the round balloon to the body. Draw on a face with a felt-tip pen. Slip the skateboarder's feet through the loops on the skateboard.

BABY

Level of Difficulty: 5+

This sculpture looks hard, but it's not that difficult if you break it down into manageable steps. It will, however, take some time.

BALLOON PROPORTIONS

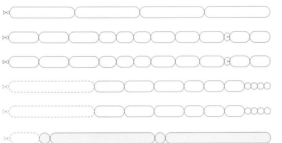

Head

1 Inflate the 11-inch round pink balloon about three-quarters full. This is the head. You can draw a face on the balloon with a felt-tip pen if you like.

Legs

2 Inflate another pink balloon, leaving 4 inches (10 cm) free at the tail. Make a medium bubble and another medium bubble, and twist lock to the knot. Make a small bubble and ear twist. This is the foot.

3 Make three medium bubbles, and twist lock the first and second bubbles. Roll lock the third bubble through these bubbles.

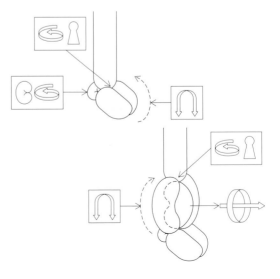

Body

4 Fully inflate another pink balloon, burp, and make a midpoint twist, and then pull the section down to make a figure eight. Force one section of the balloon through two of the balloon sections, to create the body.

5 Make three small bubbles, and twist lock the first and second bubbles. Roll lock the third bubble through the first and second bubbles. This is the knee.

6 Make three large bubbles, and twist lock the first and second bubbles. Roll lock the third bubble through the first and second bubbles. Repeat the preceding three steps and this step with a second pink balloon. These are the legs and feet.

7 To attach the legs to the body, push the long section through and twist lock through the joint at the end of the leg.

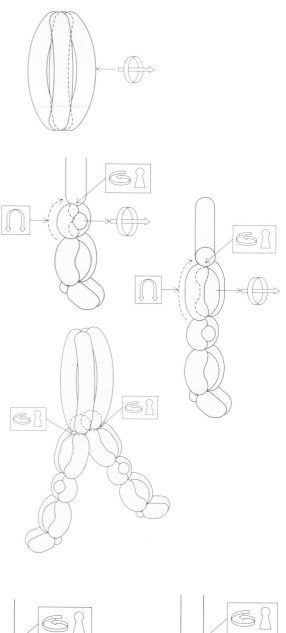

Arms

8 Inflate another pink balloon, leaving 3 to 4 inches (7.5 to 10 cm) free at the tail. Make four small bubbles, and twist lock the first and fourth bubbles. Tie the knot around the twist and twist lock. This is the hand.

9 Make three medium bubbles, and twist lock the first and second bubbles. Roll lock the third bubble through the first and second bubbles. Make elbows following the instructions in step 5, above for knees.

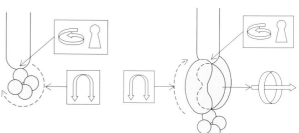

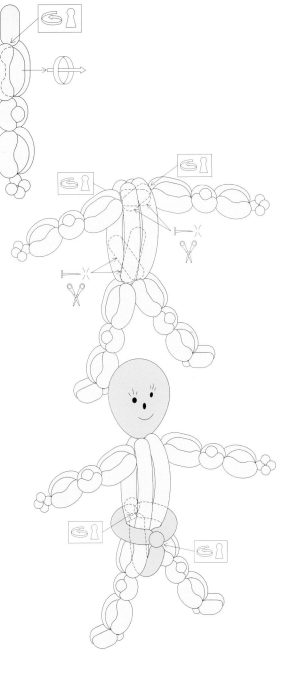

10 Make three large bubbles, and twist lock the first and second bubbles. Roll lock the third bubble though the first and second bubbles. Repeat the two previous steps and this step for the second arm and hand.

11 Join the arms to the body with the leftover balloon sections by twist locking the same way you attached the legs.

Attaching the Head

12 Attach the head to the body by twisting the mouth of the balloon to the top joints. Deflate, tie off, and trim any excess balloon.

Diaper

13 Inflate a balloon in a different color, leaving 5 inches (12.5 cm) free at the tail. Make a small bubble and wrap it around the baby's waist. Closing with a twist lock, push the balloon under the legs' and up the back. Twist lock to the other side. Make a small bubble, hold, twist, deflate, and then tie off.

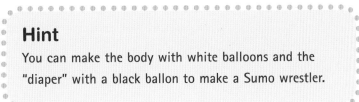

Hint
You can make the body with white balloons and the "diaper" with a black ballon to make a Sumo wrestler.

RATTLESNAKE
Level of Difficulty: 2

Shake, rattle, and twist with this reptile.

BALLOON PROPORTIONS

Rattle

1 Add about 20 grains of uncooked rice to an uninflated balloon. The rice grains are small enough to simply be fed into the balloon.

2 Inflate the balloon to about 6 inches (15 cm) and tie off. Each of the bubbles that are formed to make the rattle should contain several grains of rice. Make a small bubble and then ear twist. Make a second small bubble and ear twist. Make a third small bubble and ear twist. Make two more small bubbles, ear twisting each to hold in place. Use a turkey skewer to deflate the rest of the balloon, and tie off.

Body

3 Inflate the balloon then deflate it. This will soften up the balloon. Holding the tail end under your thumb, wrap the balloon loosely around two fingers and inflate again. Hang on as you do this and the balloon will curl. Or try using a cardboard tube to wrap the balloon around.

4 Make a small bubble, twist, and make a second small bubble, and ear twist it. Make a medium bubble, twist, and make a small bubble, then ear twist, and make a small bubble, and twist lock the knotted end with the small bubble. This is the face of the snake.

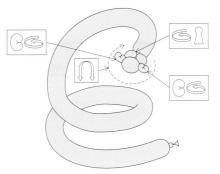

Eyes

5 Take a balloon of a contrasting color, and inflate it to about 3 to 4 inches (7.5 to 10 cm) and tie off. Twist the balloon in half. Pinch the tail of the balloon and tie off. Tie the two knotted ends together and ear twist. Attach the eyes to the snake and twist into place.

6 Wrap the rattle to the knot at the end of the snake. You can also wear this as a hat.

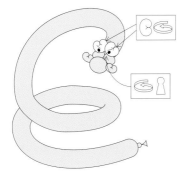

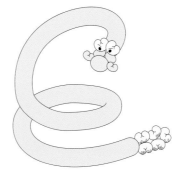

WORM
Level of Difficulty: 1

This worm won't do your garden much good, but it will make a cute hat or centerpiece. Or, drop it inside a balloon basket with the eyes peeking out. But don't wear it around your neck because this could be dangerous.

BALLOON PROPORTIONS

1 Inflate the balloon then deflate it. This will soften up the balloon. Holding the tail end under your thumb, wrap the balloon loosely around two fingers and inflate again. Hang on as you do this and the balloon will curl. Or try using a cardboard tube to wrap the balloon around.

2 Underinflate an 11-inch round balloon. With the mouth end of the balloon pointing downward, grab the balloon on either side and fold it. This will take some time, as the balloon will not want to twist. These are the eyes.

3 Twist lock the eyes to the knotted end of the balloon approximately 2 inches (5 cm) down from the end. Draw in the eyes with a felt-tip pen.

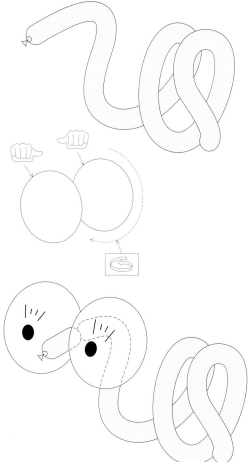

Hint
You can add two small glow sticks to the eyes and twist, making sure one glow stick is on each side.

SAXOPHONE
Level of Difficulty: 1

Other than a popping sound, balloons don't make good musical instruments, or do they?

BALLOON PROPORTIONS

1 Inflate a 6-inch geo-donut balloon, and drop an uninflated 260 balloon through the hole.

2 Inflate the balloon and squeeze some air into the tail to hold it in place.

3 Completely inflate the rest of the balloon and burp to soften. Make a small bubble and ear twist. Twist the ear twist in half to form the mouth/reed section of the sax.

4 Make a 6-inch (15-cm) bubble, small bubble, ear twist, 6-inch bubble, small bubble, and ear twist; small bubble ear twist, medium bubble, small bubble, and ear twist; then, small bubble and ear twist. Do this several times to make the keys for the sax.

5 Bend the lower end of the sax to form the upward end of the curve. Now blow your horn.

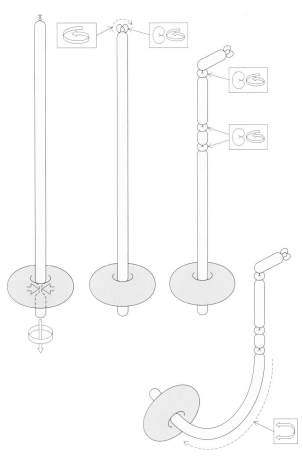

BUTTERFLY
Level of Difficulty: 1

Here's a butterfly that won't flit away.

BALLOON PROPORTIONS

1 Inflate two balloons, leaving about 3 inches (7.5 cm) free at the tail end. The balloons should be the same size.

2 Starting from the knotted end, move about 3 inches down, and holding both balloons together, twist lock. At the opposite end, grab the balloon about 4 inches (10 cm) down and twist lock. Fold this over and twist lock together at the joints. These are the wings.

3 At the tail end, choose the shorter of the two, and make a small bubble and pinch twist it. Make an ear twist from the bubble, and position it under the body of the butterfly.

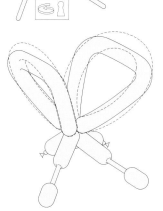

4 Make a balloon puff on the tail ends to create antennas. Do not try to make a puff by putting the end of the balloon in your mouth. You could choke on the balloon.

5 Pull on the knot and squeeze to give the balloon some extra space. Hold the loops and fold to form a triangle shape, and squeeze so that the balloons hold the butterfly-shaped wings.

BAT
Level of Difficulty: 1

If you can make the butterfly, you can make this bat.

BALLOON PROPORTIONS

1 Fully inflate two black balloons and burp them. The balloons should be the same size.

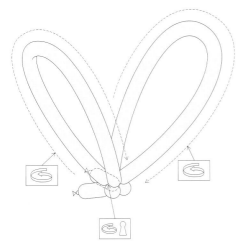

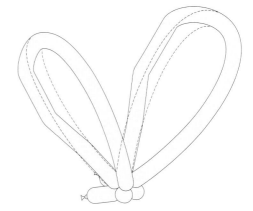

2 Starting from the knotted end, move about 2 inches (5 cm) down, and holding both balloons together, twist lock. At the opposite end, grab the balloon about 1 inch (2.5 cm) down and twist lock. These are the eyes. Fold this over and twist lock together at the joints. These are the wings. They should be egg-shaped. Hold the wings upward.

3 Grab the balloons together just above the natural curve, and squeeze together with your palms to bend the bat wings into shape. Do this again about one third from the top fold, facing away from the front curved wings. One third further down, fold toward the front curved wings.

Chapter 4
Large Creatures

OCTOPUS
Level of Difficulty: 1

One octopus, two octopuses, or octopi?
You word buffs will know that both
octopuses and octopi are correct.
Here's how to make one.

BALLOON PROPORTIONS

1 Fully inflate four balloons to the same size. Don't forget to burp the ends before tying off.

2 You might need a helper for this step. Hold all the balloons together and find the middle point. Twist all the balloons together.

3 Fold over the balloons so that the ends are all facing the same direction; take one balloon, make a medium bubble from the midpoint, then a small balloon and ear twist. Repeat with another balloon. The ear twists are the "eyes." Make sure there is one balloon between the two balloons with the "eyes" and hold them several inches down from the joint. Gather the balloons together and twist all eight arms together. Draw on some eyes with a felt-tip pen. You've got a sea creature.

SKELETON
Level of Difficulty: 4

Here's a fun decoration for Halloween.

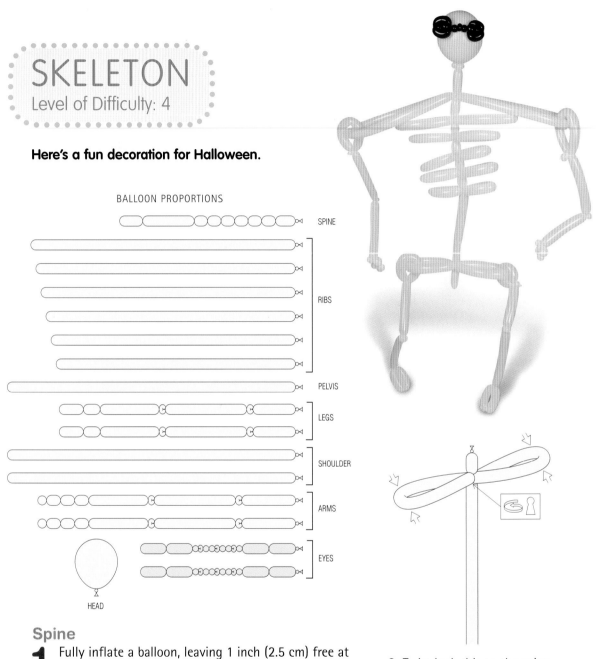

BALLOON PROPORTIONS

SPINE

RIBS

PELVIS

LEGS

SHOULDER

ARMS

EYES

HEAD

Spine

1 Fully inflate a balloon, leaving 1 inch (2.5 cm) free at the tail end.

Torso

2 Fully inflate another balloon. Squeeze the tail end and tie the mouth to the tail.

3 Make a midpoint twist and then a figure eight.

4 Twist lock this to the spine about 2 inches (5 cm) from the mouth. These are the ribs. Place end of rib between the palms of your hands and squeeze your hands together. This will give the rib a pointed shape.

5 Fully inflate another balloon, burp to soften, and tie off. Holding the knot end, lay this balloon against the first rib and twist the balloon to make it the same length. Fold over the balloon and twist tie to the knot, deflate, and tie-off to the knot. Cut off the excess. This balloon will be slightly shorter than the first one. Repeat Steps 3 and 4, joining it to the spine just above the previous balloon. The widest ribs are the top of the skeleton.

6 Repeat Step 5, with four more balloons, making each successive balloon smaller so that you create a triangle, or the shape of an inverted Christmas tree (see page 72 for Christmas Tree).

Pelvis/Legs

7 Make a full-size figure eight. Attach this to the spine about 6 inches (15 cm) down from the last rib.

8 For each leg, fully inflate a balloon. Push the mouth end of the balloon through the loop of the figure eight created on each side of the pelvis, and twist lock to hold in place.

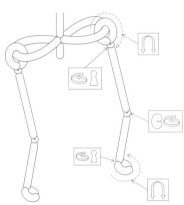

9 About halfway down the leg, make a small bubble and ear twist. This is the kneecap.

Feet

10 For each leg, make a small bubble and then a folded larger bubble and twist lock.

Shoulder and Arms

11 Fully inflate two balloons. Tie the knots and the tail ends together. Twist lock the knot and tail ends to create a large figure eight. These are the shoulders.

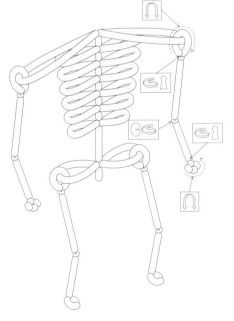

12 For each arm, fully inflate a balloon. Push the mouth end of the balloon through the loop of the figure eight created on each side of the shoulders, and twist lock to hold in place.

13 About halfway down the arm, make a small bubble and ear twist. This is the elbow.

Hand

14 Make a small bubble at the end of the balloon. Make three medium bubbles, and twist lock the last medium bubble to the small bubble. Do this for each arm.

Head

15 For the head, you will be using a raisin twist (see page 23). Insert a large wad into an 11-inch round balloon. Inflate the balloon until it is about three-quarters full.

Eyes

16 Inflate a balloon, leaving 7 inches (17.5 cm) free at the tail end.

17 Make two medium bubbles, and twist lock the medium bubbles together.

18 Make a small bubble, very small bubble, and small bubble, and roll lock these through the locked medium bubbles. Ear twist the very small bubble.

19 Make a small bubble.

20 Make a very small bubble and ear twist it.

21 Make a small bubble and then two medium bubbles, and twist lock the medium bubbles together.

22 Repeat Step 18.

23 Make a small bubble and twist, and then deflate and tie off the end.

24 Attach the eyes to the head, using a raisin twist. Place the wad where you want the eyes, and twist the eyes to the wad at the bottom of the small ear twist in the center of the eyes.

Courtesy Pioneer Balloon Company

EXTREMELY LARGE BALLOON CREATIONS—FROM BALLOON COMPETITIONS

Each year balloon professionals meet to compare notes, learn new tricks, and compete in a contest to create the biggest, coolest, or most spectacular balloon sculpture. The International Balloon Arts Convention hosts some of the best professionals in the balloon business. Perhaps this book will start you down the road to becoming a twisting artist yourself.

Dragon Sculpture
How many balloons do you think the 43 artists used to make this sculpture? The answer is in the acknowledgments.

PART III
Decorating with Balloons

Chapter 5

Table Toppers

TABLETOP FLOWERS
Level of Difficulty: 2

1 Follow the directions on page 27 to make a small vase. Instead of making a 4- inch (10-cm) base on the five spokes, make a 2- to 3-inch (5- to 7.5-cm) base, but add more rows for a taller arrangement.

Stem

2 Inflate a green balloon, leaving 4 inches free at the tail end.

3 Make a 10-inch (25-cm) bubble and twist. Add two medium bubbles and twist lock them together. This forms one leaf of the stem. Repeat to form the other leaf of the stem.

4 Make a balloon puff at the tail.

Flower

5 Fully inflate a bright-colored balloon. Remember to burp the balloon before you tie it. Squeeze the tail end of the balloon to create a ½-inch (1.5-cm) tail, and then tie the two ends together. Twist the balloon at the point directly opposite the knot. The balloon will now be evenly divided into two parts.

6 Bring the two parts together. Place one of your hands about a third of the way along the gathered balloons and twist. Then place your hand two-thirds of the way and twist. You should have three equal sections.

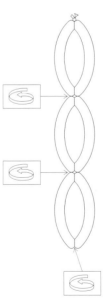

7 Fold the sections together as you would a fan. All the joints should line up. Squeeze the balloons in at the joints. Twist lock the joints together. You may need someone to help you with this. You now have a flower with six petals.

Assembling

8 Hold the stem at the balloon puff. Fold the thin neck over and into the joints of the petals so that the puff stays in the center of the petals. You now have a daisy.

9 Place the daisy into the vase.

FRUIT BASKET

No more fruit flies hovering in your kitchen with this arrangement.

1 Follow the directions on page 27 to make a small vase. You'll want one that has just a few rows so that it doesn't stand up too high on the table. Fill it with balloon fruit (see below).

Apples
Level of Difficulty: 1

Use a red, yellow, or green 321, or bee body, balloon for the apple. Inflate the balloon only about halfway, and push the knotted end halfway into the balloon using your index finger. Holding the knot, pull your finger out, and make a twist with the knot on the far side of the twist. Push the end back in, and the top of the bee stinger becomes the stem of the apple.

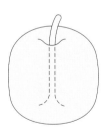

Oranges
Level of Difficulty: 1

Follow the instructions above, for making an apple but use an orange bee body balloon or a small orange round balloon.

Bananas
Level of Difficulty: 1

Blow up a yellow 260 balloon, leaving about 6 to 8 inches (15 to 20 cm) uninflated at the tail end. Fold the balloon over, and tie the mouth of the balloon to the spot where the uninflated portion of the balloon starts. Find the midpoint of the loop and twist to divide it into two sections. Find the midpoint of the new section and twist. You now have four sections. Force one of the balloons between the other two sections to make a bunch of bananas. Use a felt-tip pen to put dark spots on the banana peels.

Grapes
Level of Difficulty: 2

Inflate a purple 260 balloon to about 12 inches (30 cm), and make a series of very small bubbles. You will need 40 to 50 very small bubbles. Twist lock every five bubbles. Keep repeating this until you have run out of bubbles. Adjust and twist together to make the creation look like a bunch of grapes.

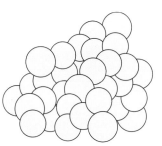

Optional: Green leaves

Inflate a green balloon about 6 inches. Make a small bubble, then four more small bubbles; twist lock the first and fifth balloon. Make another four small bubbles; twist lock the first and fourth bubble. Deflate and tie off the remainder. Attach these leaves to the grapes.

Chapter 6

Sculptures & Decorations

Christmas Theme

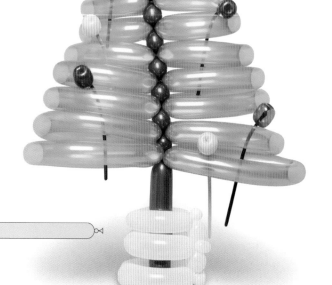

Not just for the holiday season, this is a great decoration for Arbor Day, too! You will need eleven green balloons. These will be used for the trunk and branches. You will be using a balloon of a different color for the base.

Trunk

1 Inflate one of the balloons leaving a 2-inch (5-cm) uninflated portion at the tail end. This is call the trunk.

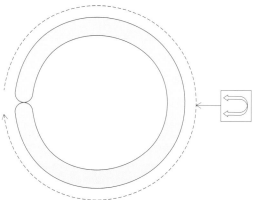

Branches

2 Take another balloon and fully inflate, burp to soften. Tie the mouth end to the tail end.

3 Make a figure eight with this balloon. Place the end of balloon between the palms of your hands, then squeeze the ends together to give them a pointed shape.

4 Twist lock this to the trunk about 8 to 10 inches (20 to 25 cm) from the mouth end of the trunk.

5 Fully inflate another balloon, burp to soften, and tie-off. Holding the knot end, lay this balloon against the previous branch and twist the balloon to make it the same length. Fold over the balloon and twist tie to the knot, deflate, and tie-off to the knot. Cut off the excess. This balloon will be slightly shorter than the first one. Repeat Steps 3 and 4, joining it to the trunk just above the previous balloon, so that you create a "Christmas tree" shape. Twist the brown balloon 2 inches above the last branch. Deflate and tie off; cut off the excess.

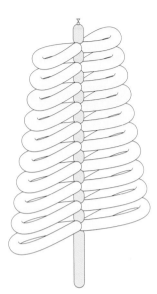

BASE

7 Inflate a new balloon in a different color. Make a small bubble, tie over the knot, and ear twist; and then make two large bubbles. Twist lock the two large bubbles together, then make a small bubble.

8 Make a small bubble, twist lock and then two large bubbles. Twist lock the two large bubbles together then make a small bubble. Repeat. You will have created three loops joined on one side and open on the other.

9 Force the trunk of the tree through the openings of the base, and you will have a standing Christmas Tree.

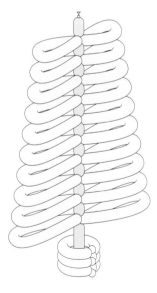

ADDING ORNAMENTS

Add ornaments by creating tulip twist bulbs in different colors and sliding the uninflated part of the balloon between the branches, or make a star following the Starfish directions on page 38. You may want to add some glow sticks to the ornaments (see page 87).

CANDY CANE
Level of Difficulty: 1

1 Fully inflate a red balloon and a white balloon, burp to soften, and twist tie these balloons together.

2 Hold one hand on the red balloon to keep it in place as you turn the white balloon. You may need a helper to rotate the balloons as you hold them.

3 When you've reached the end, twist lock into place.

4 Holding the end of the twisted balloons, fold them over your wrist several times to create the curve of the candy cane. Give this a good squeeze and it should stay in shape. Hang on a wall as a decoration.

Hint
You may want to add small bells to the candy cane.

HOLIDAY WREATH
Level of Difficulty: 1

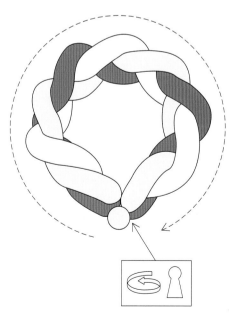

Here's a way to liven up your front door for a holiday. During the Christmas season, you could use red, green, and white balloons. For Halloween, you may want to use brown, orange, and black. For Independence Day, you could use red, white, and blue, and for spring, balloons in pastel colors.

1 Fully inflate three different colored balloons, burp to soften them, and twist tie the three balloons together.

2 Braid the balloons together, one balloon over the other, until you reach the end. Twist tie together.

3 Twist tie the front part of the braid to the end, to create a wreath.

4 Every wreath needs a bow. Fully inflate a balloon in a contrasting color and burp to soften it.

5 Fold the balloon in half, and twist lock it together at the midpoint. Take the circular part of the balloon at the midpoint, and push it down to the joint, twist locking to hold it in place.

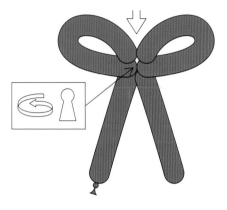

6 To attach the bow to the wreath, twist lock one of the small bubbles on the wreath to the joint on the bow. Adjust to make the wreath rounded and the bow flat.

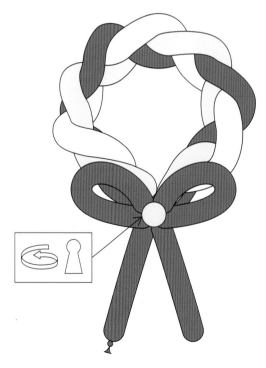

Hint

If you want a larger wreath, simply inflate and tie one or even two balloons onto the first balloons. Also, you may want to tie festive ribbons to your wreath. You can use red, white, and blue ribbons for an Independence Day wreath, or silver or gold ribbons for special occasions. If you want to make some Christmas baubles or nuts to add to your wreath, create several small tulip twist bubbles and thread them into the braid.

Chanukah Theme

MENORAH
Level of Difficulty: 3

You don't have to be Jewish to enjoy this lovely candelabra. It makes a great decoration for everyone. You'll be using three blue balloons for the base, three white balloons for the candles, and one yellow balloon for each flame.

Base

1 Fully inflate the three blue balloons, burping to soften them. Tie the balloons together at the knots. Braid the balloons about four times, and twist lock them together.

2 Make a small bubble at the end of one balloon, and fold it back up to the bottom of the braid. Twist lock it to make a loop. Repeat this step with the other two blue balloons. This will form a tripod to hold the candelabra. Use your hands to squeeze the legs into a triangle shape.

Candles

3 To make the first candle: Inflate one white balloon, leaving about 10 inches (25 cm) free at the tail end. Make a very small bubble, tie a knot to twist and ear twist, and then twist in half to make two bubbles. Make a small bubble and very small bubble and ear twist. Make another small bubble and very small bubble and ear twist.

4 To make the second candle: Make a small bubble and very small bubble and ear twist, and twist in half to make two bubbles. Make a small bubble and twist lock to the small bubble. Make a small bubble and a very small bubble and ear twist. Repeat this step to create the third and fourth candles.

5 Repeat Steps 3 and 4, using the second white balloon. Now you have the two sides of the menorah.

6 To make the tall candle in the middle: Inflate the third white balloon, leaving about 12 inches (30 cm) free at the tail end. Make a very small bubble, tie a knot to twist, and ear twist, and then twist in half to make two bubbles. Go down 8 inches (20 cm) and twist lock the two sides of the menorah to the large center candle at this joint. Deflate and tie off any remainder. With the tall balloon make a small bubble, then ear twist. Make another small bubble, ear twist. These will keep the sides in place. Make a small bubble on the bottom of the tall candle, and ear twist, and then twist in half to make two bubbles. Deflate and tie off the remainder.

7 Feed the end of the tall candle through the base, and twist lock the candle to the base at the small bubble. Use the tall candle to make a small bubble and ear twist, and another small bubble and ear twist. Deflate with a turkey skewer, tie off, and cut off the excess balloon.

Flames

For each flame, use a yellow balloon. Inflate the balloon several inches and make a small bubble and twist, and twist lock the rest of the balloon to the ear-twisted top of the candles. Deflate, tie off, and cut off the rest of the balloon.

> ## Hint
> You may want to add a small glow stick to each flame (see page 87).

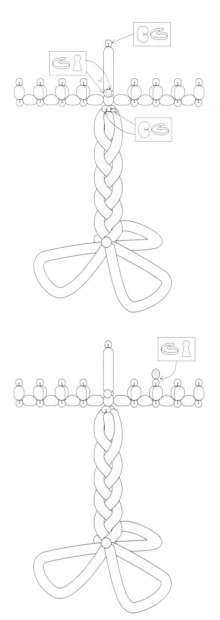

DREIDEL OR SPINNING TOP
Level of Difficulty: 3

You will need two white balloons and two blue balloons for this project.

1 Inflate the balloons, leaving about 6 inches (15 cm) free at the tail. All the balloons should be the same size.

2 Tie the knotted ends of the white balloons together. Do the same with the blue balloons.

3 Twist the knotted ends of the white balloons with the blue balloons. These will be the points of the dreidel/top.

4 Starting with one of the white balloons, make a 3-inch (7.5-cm) bubble and twist. Make a small bubble and then ear twist. Using the same balloon, make another 3-inch bubble and then twist lock it to a blue balloon. Repeat this step, joining the blue balloon to the next white balloon. Repeat again, joining the white balloon to the last blue balloon. To finish this step, join the blue balloon to the first white balloon with an ear twist.

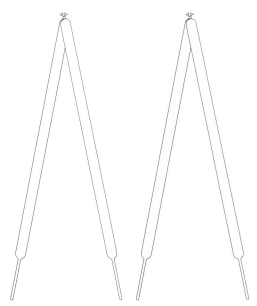

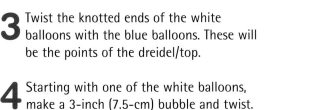

5 Position the balloons so that the long ends are all facing in the same direction, away from the point.

6 Make a bubble about 5 to 6 inches (12.5 to 15 cm) long, twist, and make a small bubble and then ear twist. Repeat Step 4, this time using the longer bubbles.

7 You should have four balloons with about the same amount left over after Step 6.

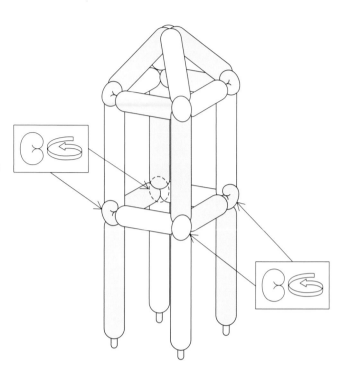

8 To make the top of the dreidel, grab the four balloons together and twist. Make a medium bubble and ear twist, and repeat three more times. Twist all the ear twists together, and you will have created the top. Pop the excess balloon and tie off. You can either trim this or use it to hang the dreidel as a decoration.

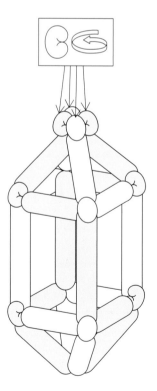

Olympics Theme

FLAME OR TORCH
Level of Difficulty: 1

Not everyone can carry the torch in the Olympics, but you can proudly and safely run with this one. As an option, you can add glow sticks to the flame.

1 For the base, use a red balloon and create a flower stem, as described in steps 2, 3, and 4 on page 67.

2 For the flames, inflate a yellow balloon, leaving 6 to 8 inches (15 to 20 cm) free at the tail. Make a small bubble, twist lock, and wrap it around itself and twist lock in place. Make a small bubble and ear twist, and another small bubble and ear twist.

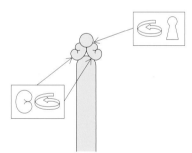

3 For the body of the flame, make a 4-inch (10-cm) bubble, two 2-inch (5-cm) bubbles, and then another 4-inch bubble, and twist lock the 4-inch bubbles together and then the 2-inch bubbles together. This will be tricky, but force the small 2-inch bubbles through the 4-inch bubbles. Using a turkey skewer, deflate the remaining balloon, pulling the excess down and tying it onto the base. Readjust the bubbles and cut off the leftover deflated balloon.

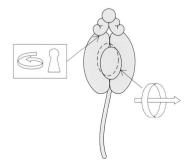

PART IV
More Fun With Balloons

Chapter 7

Putting Things
Inside Balloons

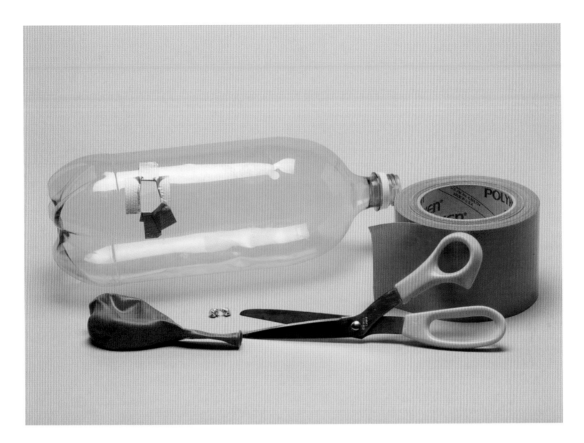

How can you place things in balloons? If you blow up a balloon and try to put something inside, the balloon will deflate and fly around the room. Professional balloon blowers have special equipment and tools they use to place objects inside, but what's a kid to do? Here's how science can help you stuff a wild balloon.

You Will Need
- large plastic bottle
- knife
- duct tape
- adult helper
- round 6-, 9-, or 11-inch balloon
- toy or object without sharp edges and smaller than the opening of the bottle.

1 Have an adult cut a small hole in the side of the bottle approximately 1 inch (2.5 cm) from the bottom. Place masking tape over the rough edges of the hole so that it won't tear the balloon.

2 Place the body of the balloon into the bottle, and fold the mouth of the balloon over the opening of the bottle.

3 Cut a piece of tape large enough to completely cover the hole you made in Step 1.

4 Partially blow up the balloon, and holding your mouth over the opening, have a helper completely cover the hole with tape. Take your mouth off the opening. The balloon should stay open and inflated. Drop the toy or object (for example, a small bell) into the opening.

5 Pull off the tape and the balloon should deflate with the object inside. Take the balloon out of the bottle, and then fully inflate it and tie off.

GLOW-IN-THE-DARK ADDITIONS

Here's a way to make some creations for Halloween look really eerie or to add a sparkling touch to a centerpiece.

You Will Need
- 1-inch-long glow sticks
- clear or white balloons

1 Feed one end of the sticks into the mouth of a clear balloon.

2 Crack the sticks to activate them.

3 Inflate the balloon to desired length to make the creation you want.

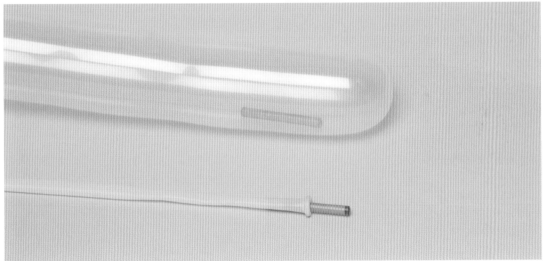

This is how to add "Glow-in-the Dark" additions to any balloon creation. The next page is how you do it for a specific creation.

GLOWING SPACE SWORD
Level of Difficulty: 1

1 Feed one end of a small glow stick into the mouth of a clear balloon.

2 Crack the stick to activate it.

3 Inflate the balloon, leaving about 3 inches (7.5 cm) free at the tail end, and tie it off.

4 Make a tulip twist at the mouth end of the balloon. Make a medium bubble, small bubble, and another medium bubble, and twist lock the medium bubbles together. This is one side of the handle. Repeat this step for the second side of the handle. Do this again for the third side.

5 Ear twist each of the small bubbles on each side of the handle. You now have a glowing space sword.

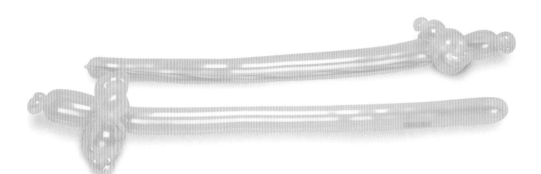

PUTTING YOUR TALENTS TO USE

You can make all these creatures, so now what?
Here are some ideas.

Make balloon creatures for a school fair or entertain
children at a hospital. You can volunteer at various
functions and demonstrate your artistry for the enjoyment
of others. If you get good enough, you can even earn extra
money by performing at birthday parties.

Did you know that NASA's Jet Propulsion Lab sponsors a
balloon car contest? Budding engineers design vehicles
that use "official" balloons to power a car over a specially
designed course. Check the NASA Web site for more
details.

Index

About the Authors

MICHAEL OUCHI learned how to twist balloons and many other busking skills on the staff at the 1987 Edmonton Street Performer's Festival. Since then he has performed at festivals and events in Alberta, British Columbia, Hawaii, Yukon Territories, and Washington State. Highlights include the Calgary International Children's Festival, First Night Honolulu, and premiered at the Yukon International Storytelling Festival his interactive storytelling show, "Tales from the Latex Skirt," in which audience members and balloon creations become the characters in amazing and hilarious tales. Michael lives in North Vancouver with his wife Tracy and son Maxwell. He is a computer software trainer and consultant by training and profession.

Vancouver author SHAR LEVINE is an internationally award-winning, best selling author of children's science books and science toys/kits. She has written over 50 books and with her co-author and best friend, Leslie Johnstone, has just won the prestigious 2006 Eve Savory Award for Science Communication from the BC Innovation Council. Their book, *Backyard Science* (2005), was chosen as one of the best books of the year by Science Books and Films and was short-listed for the Subaru Prize (hands-on activity books) from the American Association for the Advancement of Science. Other recent books include *First Science Experiments: The Amazing Human Body, First Science Experiments: Magnet Power.* Shar and Michael Ouchi collaborated before on their previous Sterling Publishing title *The Ultimate Balloon Book.*